Paths to Power

By

A. W. Tozer

CHRISTIAN PUBLICATIONS, INC.

3825 Hartzdale Drive, Camp Hill, PA 17011
www.christianpublications.com

Faithful, biblical publishing since 1883

Paths to Power
ISBN: 0-87509-190-3
Copyright by Christian Publications, Inc.
All rights reserved
Printed in the United States of America

02   03   04   05   06   6   5   4   3   2

Contents

FOREWORD

We present in these pages an outline which
may at least serve to suggest the way to
greater spiritual power for many of us. Or, as
the title intimates, each major idea may be a
"path" leading to a life of abundant grace
promised in the Sacred Word. Let us remember
that a path is merely a way toward something;
it can never be the thing itself. A knowledge of
the truth is not enough; the truth must be followed if we would realize in actual experience
the blessedness which is here described.

1

Power in Action

The greatest event in history was the coming of Jesus Christ into the world to live and to die for mankind. The next greatest event was the going forth of the Church to embody the life of Christ and to spread the knowledge of His salvation throughout the earth.

It was not an easy task which the Church faced when she came down from that upper room. To carry on the work of a man who was known to have died—to have died as criminals die—and more than that, to persuade others that this man had risen again from the dead and that He was the Son of God and Saviour: this mission was, in the nature of it, doomed to failure from the start. Who would credit such a fantastic story? Who would put faith in one whom society had condemned and crucified? Left to herself the Church must have perished as a thousand abortive sects had done before her, and have left nothing for a future generation to remember.

That the Church did not so perish was due entirely to the miraculous element within her. That element was supplied by the Holy Spirit who came at Pentecost to empower her for her task. For the Church was not an organization merely, not a movement, but a walking incarnation of spiritual energy. And she accomplished within a few brief years such prodigies of moral conquest as to leave us wholly without an explanation—apart from God.

In short, the Church began in power, moved in power and moved just as long as she had power. When she no longer had power she dug in for safety and sought to conserve her gains. But her blessings were like the manna: when they tried to keep it overnight it bred worms and stank. So we have had monasticism, scholasticism, institutionalism; and they have all been indicative of the same thing: absence of spiritual power. In Church history every return to New Testament power has marked a new advance somewhere, a fresh proclamation of the gospel, an upsurge of missionary zeal; and every diminution of power has seen the rise of some new mechanism for conservation and defense.

If this analysis is reasonably correct, then we are today in a state of very low spiritual energy: for it cannot be denied that the modern Church has dug in up to her ears and is struggling desperately to defend the little ground she holds. She lacks the spiritual insight to know that her best defense is an offense, and she is too languid to put the knowledge into effect if she had it.

If we are to advance we must have power. Paganism is slowly closing in on the Church, and her only response is an occasional "drive" for one thing or another—usually money—or a noisy but timid campaign to improve the morals of the movies. Such activities amount to little more than a slight twitching of the muscles of a drowsy giant too sleepy to care. These efforts sometimes reach the headlines, but they accomplish little that is lasting, and are soon forgotten. The Church must have power; she must become formidable, a moral force to be reckoned with, if she would regain her lost position of spiritual ascendancy and make her message the revolutionizing, conquering thing it once was.

Since "power" is a word of many uses and

misuses, let me explain what I mean by it. First, I mean spiritual energy of sufficient voltage to produce great saints once again. That breed of mild, harmless Christian grown in our generation is but a poor sample of what the grace of God can do when it operates in power in a human heart. The emotionless act of "accepting the Lord" practiced among us bears little resemblance to the whirlwind conversions of the past. We need the power that transforms, that fills the soul with a sweet intoxication, that will make a former persecutor to be "beside himself" with the love of Christ. We have today theological saints who can (and must) be proved to be saints by an appeal to the Greek original. We need saints whose lives proclaim their sainthood, and who need not run to the concordance for authentication.

Secondly, I mean a spiritual unction that will give a heavenly unction to our worship, that will make our meeting places sweet with the divine Presence. In such a holy place showy sermons and streamlined personalities will be all out of order, a very grief to the Holy Spirit, and the emphasis will fall where it belongs, upon the Lord Himself and His message to mankind.

Then, I mean that heavenly quality which

marks the Church as a divine thing. The greatest proof of our weakness these days is that there is no longer anything terrible or mysterious about us. The Church has been explained—the surest evidence of her fall. We now have little that cannot be accounted for by psychology and statistics. In that early Church they met together on Solomon's porch, and so great was the sense of God's presence that "no man durst join himself to them." The world saw fire in that bush and stood back in fear; but no one is afraid of ashes. Today they dare come as close as they please. They even slap the professed bride of Christ on the back and get coarsely familiar. If we ever again impress unsaved men with a wholesome fear of the supernatural we must have once more the dignity of the Holy Spirit; we must know again that awe-inspiring mystery which comes upon men and churches when they are full of the power of God.

Again, I mean that effective energy which God has, both in biblical and in post-biblical times, released into the Church and into the circumstances surrounding her, which made her fruitful in labor and invincible before her foes. Miracles? Yes, when and where they were necessary. Answers to prayer? Special providences? All of these and more. It is all summed up in the words of the Evangelist Mark: "And they went forth, and preached every where, the Lord working with them, and confirming the words with signs following." The whole Book of Acts and the noblest chapters of Church history since New Testament times are but an extension of that verse.

Such words as those in the second chapter of Hebrews stand as a rebuke to the unbelieving Christians of our day: "God also bearing them witness, both with signs and wonders, and with divers miracles, and gifts of the Holy Ghost, according to his own will." A cold Church is forced to "interpret" such language. She cannot enter into it, so she explains it away. Not a little juggling is required, and not a few statements for which there is no scriptural authority, but anything will do to save face and justify our half-dead condition. Such defensive exegesis is but a refuge for unbelieving orthodoxy, a hiding place for a Church too weak to stand.

No one with a knowledge of the facts can deny the need for supernatural aid in the work of world evangelization. We are so hopelessly outclassed by the world's superior strength that for us it means either God's help or sure defeat. The Christian who goes out without faith in "wonders" will return without fruit. No one dare be so rash as to seek to do impossible things unless he has first been empowered by the God of the impossible. "The power of the Lord was there" is our guarantee of victory.

Lastly, by *power* I mean that divine afflatus which moves the heart and persuades the hearer to repent and believe in Christ. It is not eloquence; it is not logic; it is not argument. It is not any of these things, though it may accompany any or all of them. It is more penetrating than thought, more disconcerting than conscience, more convincing than reason. It is the subtle *wonder* that follows anointed preaching, a mysterious operation of spirit on spirit. Such power must be present in some degree before anyone can be saved. It is the ultimate enabling without which the most earnest seeker must fall short of true saving faith.

Everything else being equal, we shall have as much success in Christian work as we have power, no more and no less. Lack of fruit over a period argues lack of power as certainly as the sparks fly upward. Outward circumstances may hinder for a time, but nothing can long stand against the naked power of God. As well

try to fight the jagged lightning as to oppose
this power when it is released upon men. Then
it will either save or destroy; it will give life or
bring death.

"Ye shall receive power" is God's promise
and God's provision. The rest waits on us.

2

God's Part and Man's

Failure to distinguish the part of God from the part of man in salvation has prevented countless seekers from finding peace, and left whole sections of the Church of Christ powerless for long periods of time.

Let it be boldly stated that there are some things which only God can do, and for us to attempt to do them is to waste our efforts; and there are other things which only man can do, and for us to ask God to do them is to waste our prayers. It is vain for us to try to do the work which can only be done by sovereign grace; it is equally vain for us to implore God to do what has been commanded by sovereign authority.

Among the things which only God can do, of first importance to us is the work of redemption. Atonement was accomplished in that holy place where none but a divine Saviour could come. That glorious work owes nothing to the effort of any man; the best of Adam's race could add nothing there. It was all of God, and man could simply have no part.

Redemption is an objective fact. It is a work potentially saving, wrought for man, but done independent of and exterior to the individual. Christ's work on Calvary made atonement for every man, but it did not save any man.

Salvation is personal. It is redemption made effective toward the individual. Salvation is the work of God in the heart, made possible by the work of God on the Cross. Both the once-done work of redemption and the many-times-multiplied work of salvation are in the class of things which only God can do. No man can forgive his own sins; no man can regenerate his own heart; no man can declare himself justified and clean. All this is the work of God *in* man, flowing out of the work which Christ has already done *for* man. Universal atonement makes salvation universally available, but it does not make it universally effective toward the individual.

If atonement was made for all men, why are not all saved? The answer is that *before re-*

16

demption becomes effective toward the individual man there is an act which that man must do. That act is not one of merit, but of condition. And it is an act of eternal importance to us because its non-fulfillment prevents us from receiving the effective work of Christ in personal salvation. This act of appropriating salvation is one which *only man can do.*

The orthodoxy of our day is afraid to face this truth. We have been schooled in the doctrine of grace, and we fear to state things so baldly lest we rob grace of its glory and detract from the finished work of Christ. But it is a mistake to speak softly on a subject so vital to the soul. We should get the distinction clear and then be as bold as the truth compels us to be. We need not fear that we shall steal away the glory of God by honoring the truth He Himself has revealed. Failure to distinguish God's part from man's has resulted in mental confusion and moral inaction among Christians. Assurance and power require that we know and do the truth as revealed to us in the Sacred Word.

In the things-which-God-cannot-do category is this: *God cannot do our repenting for us.* In our efforts to magnify grace we have so preached the truth as to convey the impression that repentance is a work of God. This is a grave mistake, and one which is taking a frightful toll among Christians everywhere. God has commanded all men to repent. It is a work which only they can do. It is morally impossible for one person to repent for another. Even Christ could not do this. He could die for us, but He cannot do our repenting for us.

God in His mercy may "incline" us to repent and by His inworking Spirit assist us to repent; but before we can be saved we must of our own free will repent toward God and believe in Jesus Christ. This the Bible plainly teaches; this experience abundantly supports. Repentance involves moral reformation. The wrong practices are on man's part, and only man can correct them. Lying, for instance, is an act of man, and one for which he must accept full responsibility. When he repents he will quit lying. God will not quit for him; he will quit for himself.

When stated thus frankly everything seems obvious enough, and we may wonder how reasonable persons could expect someone else to relieve them of their personal obligation to repent. In practice, however, and under the pressure of strong religious emotion, things are not so plain as one might suppose. The fact is, the "all has been done, you can do nothing" emphasis has caused no end of confusion among seekers everywhere. People are told they must surely perish because of what they *are,* not because of what they *do;* what they do does not enter into the picture at all. And furthermore, they can do nothing in the direction of salvation; even to suggest such a thing is to offend God: is not the horrible example of Cain enough to prove that? So they are tossed helplessly between the first Adam and the last Adam. One did their sinning for them and the other has done everything else. Thus the nerve of their moral life is cut and they sink back in despair, afraid to move lest they be guilty of sinful self-effort. At the same time they are deeply troubled with the knowledge that there is something seriously wrong with their religious lives. The remedy is to see clearly that men are not lost because of what someone did thousands of years ago; *they are lost because they sin individually and in person.* We will never be judged for Adam's sin, but for our own. For our own sins we are and must remain fully responsible until they have been brought for disposition to the Cross of Jesus. The idea that we can delegate repentance is an erroneous inference drawn from the doctrine of grace wrongly presented and imperfectly understood.

Another thing God cannot do: *He cannot believe for us.* Faith is a gift of God, to be sure, but whether or not we shall act upon that faith lies altogether within our own power. We may or we may not, as we choose. True belief requires that we change our attitude toward God. It means that we not only acknowledge His trustworthiness but go on to trust His promises and obey His commandments. That is Bible faith; anything less is self-deception. Where God is the object of faith He cannot be the subject also. The repentant sinner is the subject, and as such he must put his faith in Christ as his Saviour. This he must do for himself. God may help him, He may wait long and be patient, but He can never take his place and do the act for him.

The day when it is once more understood that God will not be responsible for our sin and unbelief will be a glad one for the Church of Christ. The realization that we are personally responsible for our individual sins may be a shock to our hearts, but it will clear the air and remove the uncertainty. Returning sinners waste their time begging God to perform the very acts He has sternly commanded them to do. He will not argue with them; He will simply leave them to their disappointment. Unbelief is a great sin; or more accurately stated, *it is an evidence of sins unconfessed.* Repent and believe is the order. Faith will follow repentance, and salvation will be the outcome.

Any interpretation of free grace which relieves the sinner of responsibility to repent is not of God nor in accordance with revealed truth. Nor is God responsible to help us to repent. He owes us nothing but justice. The only man who actually gets his just deserts is the man who dies in sin and goes unblessed to judgment. All others are objects of unearned mercy. To wait for God to help us to repent, or to believe that He is morally obliged to do so, is to misunderstand the whole plan of salvation.

Just what has all this to do with the lack of power in our churches? Very much indeed. Millions begin their religious lives without understanding their moral duty to God. They try to believe without having first repented. They try to have faith without intending to bring their lives into moral conformity with the will of God. Consequently they are not clear about anything. They are full of doubts and hidden perplexities. They are secretly disappointed with their lives, and are for the most part joyless and without enthusiasm. It is hard to extract much delight from uncertainty.

There is no use exhorting such would-be Christians to seek power; no use talking to them about the surrendered life. They simply cannot understand it. They listen to the sermon and then go their way, waiting in vain for God to do the things He has commanded *them* to do. Until this is corrected we can hope for very little power in our churches.

3

The Fruits of Obedience

To obey, in New Testament usage, means to give earnest attention to the Word, to submit to its authority, and to carry out its instructions.

Obedience in this sense is almost a dead letter in modern Christianity. It may be taught now and then in a languid sort of way, but it is not stressed sufficiently to give it power over the lives of the hearers. For, to become effective, a doctrine must not only be received and held by the Church, but must have behind it such pressure of moral conviction that the emphasis will fall like a blow upon a percussion cap, setting off the energy latent within.

The Church of our day has soft-pedaled the doctrine of obedience, either neglecting it altogether or mentioning it only apologetically and without urgency. This results from a fundamental confusion of obedience with works in the minds of preacher and people. To escape the error of salvation by works we have fallen into the opposite error of salvation without obedience. In our eagerness to get rid of the legalistic doctrine of works we have thrown out the baby with the bath and gotten rid of obedience as well.

The Bible knows nothing of salvation apart from obedience. Paul testified that he was sent to preach "obedience to the faith among all nations." He reminded the Roman Christians that they had been set free from sin because they had "obeyed from the heart that form of doctrine which was delivered you." In the New Testament there is no contradiction between faith and obedience. Between faith and law-works, yes; between law and grace, yes; but between faith and obedience, not at all. The Bible recognizes no faith that does not lead to obedience, nor does it recognize any obedience that does not spring from faith. The two are opposite sides of the same coin. Were we to split a coin edgewise we would destroy both sides and render the whole thing valueless. So faith and obedience are forever joined and each one is without value when separated from the other.

24

The trouble with many of us today is that we are trying to believe without intending to obey.

The message of the Cross contains two elements: (1) Promises and declarations to be believed, and (2) commandments to be obeyed. Obviously faith is necessary to the first and obedience to the second. The only thing we can do with a promise or statement of fact is to believe it; it is physically impossible to obey it, for it is not addressed to the will, but to the understanding. It is equally impossible to believe a command; it is not addressed to our understanding, but to our will. True, we may have faith in its justice; we may have confidence that it is a good and right command, but that is not enough. Until we have either obeyed or refused to obey we have not done anything about it yet. To strain to exercise faith toward that which is addressed to our obedience is to get ourselves tangled in a maze of impossibilities.

The doctrine of Christ crucified and the wealth of truths which cluster around it have in them this dual content. So the apostle could speak of "obedience to the faith" without talking contradictions. And it can be said, "The gospel is the power of God unto salvation to everyone that *believeth,*" and "He became the author of eternal salvation unto all them that *obey* him." There is nothing incompatible between these statements when they are understood in the light of the essential unity of faith and obedience.

The weakness in our message today is our overemphasis on faith with a corresponding underemphasis on obedience. This has been carried so far that "believe" has been made to double for "obey" in the minds of millions of religious persons. The result is a host of mental Christians whose characters are malformed and whose lives are all out of proportion. Imagination has been mistaken for faith, and belief has been robbed of its moral content and made to be little more than an assent to gospel truth. And all this in the name of orthodoxy.

There is a mental disease fairly familiar to all of us where the patient lives in a world wholly imaginary. It is a play-world, a world of pure fancy, with no objective reality corresponding to it. Everyone knows this except the patient himself. He will argue for his world with all the logic of a sane man, and the pathetic thing is that he is utterly sincere. So we find Christians who have lived so long in the rarified air of imagination that it seems next to impossible to relate them to reality. Non-obedience has paralyzed their moral legs and dissolved their backbones, and they slump down in a spongy heap of religious theory, believing everything ardently, but obeying nothing at all. Indeed, they are deeply shocked at the very mention of the word "obey." To them it smacks of heresy and self-righteousness and is the result of failure to rightly divide the word of truth. Their doctrine of supine inaction is New Testament religion! It is the truth for which the Reformers died! Everything else is legalism and the religion of Cain.

All this we might pass over as merely one more of those things were it not that this creed of the moral impasse has influenced practically every corner of the Christian world, has captured Bible schools, has determined the content of evangelistic preaching, and has gone far to decide what kind of Christians we all shall be. Without doubt the popular misconception of the function of faith, and the failure of our teachers to insist upon obedience, have weakened the Church and retarded revival tragically in the last half-century. The only cure is to remove the cause. This will take some courage, but it will be worth the labor.

We are always in danger of falling victim to words. An unctuous phrase may easily take the place of spiritual reality. One example is the expression "Following the Lord," so often used among Christians, or its variation, "Following the Lamb." We overlook the fact that this cannot be taken literally. We cannot now, as those first disciples could, follow the Master over a given geographical area. We tend to think of it literally but at the same time *feel* its literal impossibility, with the result that it has come to mean little more than a nodded agreement to the truths of Christianity. It may startle us to learn that "following" is a New Testament word used to cover the idea of an established habit of obedience to the commandments of Christ.

Look at the fruits of obedience as described in the New Testament: The house of the obedient man is builded upon a rock (Matt. 7:24). He shall be loved by the Father and shall have the manifestation of the Father and the Son, who will come unto him and make their abode with him (John 14:21, 23). He shall abide in the love of Christ (John 15:10). By obedience to the doctrines of Christ he is set free from sin and made a servant of righteousness (Rom. 6:17, 18). The Holy Spirit is given to him (Acts 5:32). He is delivered from self-deception and blessed in his deeds (James 1:22-25). His faith is perfected (James 2:22). He is confirmed in his assurance toward God and given confidence in prayer, so that what he asks is given to him (1 John 3:18-22). These are only a few among the many verses that may be cited from the New Testament. But more to the point than any number of proof texts is the fact that *the whole drift of the New Testament is in that direction.* One or two texts might be misunderstood, but there is no mistaking the whole tenor of Scripture.

What does all this add up to? What are its practical implications for us today? Just that the power of God is at our disposal, waiting for us to call it into action by meeting the conditions which are plainly laid down. God is ready to send down floods of blessing upon us as we begin to obey His plain instructions. We need no new doctrine, no new movement, no "key," no imported evangelist or expensive "course" to show us the way. It is before us as clear as a four-lane highway.

To any inquirer I would say, "Just do the next thing you know you should do to carry out the will of the Lord. If there is sin in your life, quit it instantly. Put away lying, gossiping, dishonesty, or whatever your sin may be. Forsake worldly pleasures, extravagance in spending, vanity in dress, in your car, in your home. Get right with any person you may have wronged. Forgive everyone who may have wronged you. Begin to use your money to help the poor and advance the cause of Christ. Take up the Cross and live sacrificially. Pray, attend the Lord's services. Witness for Christ, not only when it is convenient but when you know you should. Look to no cost and fear no consequences. Study the Bible to learn the will of God and then do His will as you understand it. Start now by doing the next thing, and then go on from there."

4

Miracles Follow the Plow

"Break up your fallow ground: for it is time to seek the Lord, till he come and rain righteousness upon you" (Hos. 10: 12).

Here are two kinds of ground: fallow ground, and ground that has been broken up by the plow.

The fallow field is smug, contented, protected from the shock of the plow and the agitation of the harrow. Such a field, as it lies year after year, becomes a familiar landmark to the crow and the blue jay. Had it intelligence, it might take a lot of satisfaction in its reputation; it has stability; nature has adopted it; it can be counted upon to remain always the same while the fields around it change from brown to green and back to brown again. Safe and undisturbed, it sprawls lazily in the sunshine, the picture of sleepy contentment. But it is paying a terrible price for its tranquility: Never does it see the miracle of growth; never does it feel the motions of mounting life nor see the wonders of bursting seed nor the beauty of ripening grain. Fruit it can never know because it is afraid of the plow and the harrow.

In direct opposite to this, the cultivated field has yielded itself to the adventure of living. The protecting fence has opened to admit the plow, and the plow has come as plows always come, practical, cruel, business-like and in a hurry. Peace has been shattered by the shouting farmer and the rattle of machinery. The field has felt the travail of change; it has been upset, turned over, bruised and broken, but its rewards come hard upon its labors. The seed shoots up into the daylight its miracle of life, curious, exploring the new world above it. All over the field the hand of God is at work in the age-old and ever renewed service of creation. New things are born, to grow, mature, and consummate the grand prophecy latent in the seed when it entered the ground. Nature's wonders follow the plow.

There are two kinds of lives also: the fallow and the plowed. For examples of the fallow life we need not go far. They are all too plentiful among us.

The man of fallow life is contented with himself and the fruit he once bore. He does not want to be disturbed. He smiles in tolerant superiority at revivals, fastings, self-searchings, and all the travail of fruit bearing and the anguish of advance. The spirit of adventure is dead within him. He is steady, "faithful," always in his accustomed place (like the old field), conservative, and something of a landmark in the little church. But he is fruitless. The curse of such a life is that it is fixed, both in size and in content. *To be* has taken the place of *to become*. The worst that can be said of such a man is that he *is* what he *will be*. He has fenced himself in, and by the same act he has fenced out God and the miracle.

The plowed life is the life that has, in the act of repentance, thrown down the protecting fences and sent the plow of confession into the soul. The urge of the Spirit, the pressure of circumstances and the distress of fruitless living have combined thoroughly to humble the heart. Such a life has put away defense, and has forsaken the safety of death for the peril of life. Discontent, yearning, contrition, courageous obedience to the will of God: these have

33

bruised and broken the soil till it is ready again for the seed. And as always fruit follows the plow. Life and growth begin as God "rains down righteousness." Such a one can testify, "And the hand of the Lord was upon me there."

Corresponding to these two kinds of life, religious history shows two phases, the dynamic and the static.

The dynamic periods were those heroic times when God's people stirred themselves to do the Lord's bidding and went out fearlessly to carry His witness to the world. They exchanged the safety of inaction for the hazards of God-inspired progress. Invariably the power of God followed such action. The miracle of God went when and where His people went; it stayed when His people stopped.

The static periods were those times when the people of God tired of the struggle and sought a life of peace and security. Then they busied themselves trying to conserve the gains made in those more daring times when the power of God moved among them.

Bible history is replete with examples. Abraham "went out" on his great adventure of faith, and God went with him. Revelations, theophanies, the gift of Palestine, covenants and promises of rich blessings to come were the result. Then Israel went down into Egypt, and the wonders ceased for four hundred years. At the end of that time Moses heard the call of God and stepped forth to challenge the oppressor. A whirlwind of power accompanied that challenge, and Israel soon began to march. As long as she dared to march God sent out His miracles to clear the way for her. Whenever she lay down like a fallow field He turned off His blessing and waited for her to rise again and command His power.

This is a brief but fair outline of the history of Israel and of the Church as well. As long as they "went forth and preached everywhere," the Lord worked "with them, . . . confirming the word with signs following." But when they retreated to monasteries or played at building pretty cathedrals, the help of God was withdrawn till a Luther or a Wesley arose to challenge hell again. Then invariably God poured out His power as before.

In every denomination, missionary society, local church or individual Christian this law operates. God works as long as His people *live daringly:* He ceases when they no longer need His aid. As soon as we seek protection out of God, we find it to our own undoing. Let us build a safety-wall of endowments, by-laws, prestige, multiplied agencies for the delegation of our duties, and creeping paralysis sets in at once, a paralysis which can only end in death.

The power of God comes only where it is called out by the plow. It is released into the Church only when she is doing something that demands it. By the word "doing" I do not mean mere activity. The Church has plenty of "hustle" as it is, but in all her activities she is very careful to leave her fallow ground mostly untouched. She is careful to confine her hustling within the fear-marked boundaries of complete safety. That is why she is fruitless; she is safe, but fallow.

Look around today and see where the miracles of power are taking place. Never in the seminary where each thought is prepared for the student, to be received painlessly and at second hand; never in the religious institution where tradition and habit have long ago made faith unnecessary; never in the old church where memorial tablets plastered over the furniture bear silent testimony to a glory that once was. Invariably where daring faith is struggling to advance against hopeless odds, there is God sending "help from the sanctuary."

In the missionary society with which I have for many years been associated I have noticed that the power of God has always hovered over our frontiers. Miracles have accompanied our advances and have ceased when and where we allowed ourselves to become satisfied and ceased to advance. The creed of power can not save a movement from barrenness. There must be also the work of power.

But I am more concerned with the effect of this truth upon the local church and the individual. Look at that church where plentiful fruit was once the regular and expected thing, but now there is little or no fruit, and the power of God seems to be in abeyance. What is the trouble? God has not changed, nor has His purpose for that church changed in the slightest measure. No, the church itself has changed.

A little self-examination will reveal that it and its members have become fallow. It has lived through its early travails and has now come to accept an easier way of life. It is content to carry on its painless program with enough money to pay its bills and a membership large enough to assure its future. Its members now look to it for security rather than for guidance in the battle between good and evil. It has become a school instead of a barracks. Its members are students, not soldiers. They study the experiences of others instead of seeking new experiences of their own.

The only way to power for such a church is to come out of hiding and once more take the danger-encircled path of obedience. Its security is its deadliest foe. The church that fears the plow writes its own epitaph: the church that uses the plow walks in the way of revival.

5

Doctrinal Hindrances

To any casual observer of the religious scene
today, two things will at once be evident: one,
that there is very little sense of sin among the
unsaved, and two, that the average professed
Christian lives a life so worldly and careless
that it is difficult to distinguish him from the
unconverted man. The power that brings conviction to the sinner and enables the Christian
to overcome in daily living is being hindered
somewhere. It would be oversimplification to
name any one thing as the alone cause, for
many things stand in the way of the full realization of our New Testament privileges. There
is one class of hindrances, however, which
stands out so conspicuously that we are safe in
attributing to it a very large part of our trouble. I mean wrong doctrines or overemphasis

on right ones. I want to point out some of these doctrines, and I do it with the earnest hope that it may not excite controversy, but bring us rather to a reverent examination of our position.

Fundamental Christianity in our times is deeply influenced by that ancient enemy of righteousness, antinomianism. The creed of the antinomian is easily stated: We are saved by faith alone; works have no place in salvation; conduct is works, and is therefore of no importance. What we *do* cannot matter as long as we believe rightly. The divorce between creed and conduct is absolute and final. The question of sin is settled by the Cross; conduct is outside the circle of faith and cannot come between the believer and God. Such, in brief, is the teaching of the antinomian. And so fully has it permeated the Fundamental element in modern Christianity that it is accepted by the religious masses as the very truth of God.

Antinomianism is the doctrine of grace carried by uncorrected logic to the point of absurdity. It takes the teaching of justification by faith and twists it into deformity. It plagued the Apostle Paul in the early Church and called out some of his most picturesque denunciations. When the question is asked, "Shall we continue in sin that grace may abound?" he answers *no* with that terrific argument in the sixth chapter of Romans.

The advocates of antinomianism in our times deserve our respect for at least one thing: their motive is good. Their error springs from their very eagerness to magnify grace and exalt the freedom of the gospel. They start right, but allow themselves to be carried beyond what is written by a slavish adherence to undisciplined logic. It is always dangerous to isolate a truth and then press it to its limit without regard to other truths. It is not the teaching of the Scriptures that grace makes us free to do evil. Rather, it sets us free to do good. Between these two conceptions of grace there is a great gulf fixed. It may be stated as an axiom of the Christian system that whatever makes sin permissible is a foe of God and an enemy of the souls of men.

Right after the first World War there broke out an epidemic of popular evangelism with the emphasis upon what was called the "positive" gospel. The catch-words were "believe," "program," "vision." The outlook was wholly objective. Men fulminated against duty, commandments and what they called scornfully "a decalogue of don'ts." They talked about a "big," "lovely" Jesus who had come to help us poor but well-meaning sinners to get the victory. Christ was presented as a powerful but not too particular Answerer of Prayer. The message was so presented as to encourage a loaves-and-fishes attitude toward Christ. That part of the New Testament which acts as an incentive toward holy living was carefully edited out. It was said to be "negative" and was not tolerated. Thousands sought help who had no desire to leave all and follow the Lord. The will of God was interpreted as "Come and get it." Christ thus became a useful convenience, but His indisputable claim to Lordship over the believer was tacitly cancelled out.

Much of this is now history. The economic depression of the thirties helped to end it by making the huge meetings which propagated it unprofitable. But its evil fruits remain. The stream of gospel thought had been fouled, and its waters are still muddy. One thing that remains as a dangerous hangover from those gala days is the comfortable habit of blaming everything on the devil. No one was supposed to feel any personal guilt; the devil had done it, so why blame the sinner for the devil's misdeeds? He became the universal scapegoat, to take the blame for every bit of human deviltry from Adam to the present day. One gathered that we genial and lovable sinners are not really bad; we are merely led astray by the blandishments of that mischievous old Puck of the heavenly places. Our sins are not the expression of our rebellious wills; they are only bruises where the devil has been kicking us around. Of course sinners can feel no guilt, seeing they are merely the victims of another's wickedness.

Under that kind of teaching there can be no self-condemnation, but there can be, and is, plenty of self-pity over the raw deal we innocent sinners got at the hand of the devil. Now, no Bible student will underestimate the sinister work of Satan, but to make him responsible for our sins is to practice deadly deception upon ourselves. And the hardest deception to cure is that which is self-imposed.

Another doctrine which hinders God's work, and one which is heard almost everywhere, is that sinners are not lost because they have sinned, but because they have not accepted Jesus. "Men are not lost because they murder; they are not sent to hell because they lie and steal and blaspheme; they are sent to hell because they reject a Saviour." This short-sighted preachment is thundered at us constantly, and is seldom challenged by the hearers. A parallel argument would be hooted down as silly, but apparently no one notices it: "That man with a cancer is dying, but it is not the cancer that is killing him; it is his failure to accept a cure." Is it not plain that the only reason the man would need a cure is that he is already marked for death by the cancer? The only reason I need a Saviour, in His capacity as Saviour, is that I am already marked for hell by the sins I have committed. Refusing to believe in Christ is a symptom of deeper evil in the life, of sins unconfessed and wicked ways unforsaken. The guilt lies in acts of sin; the proof of that guilt is seen in the rejection of the Saviour.

If anyone should feel like brushing this aside as mere verbal sparring, let him first pause: the doctrine that the only damning sin is the rejection of Jesus is definitely a contributing cause of our present weakness and lack of moral grip. It is nothing but a neat theological sophism which has become identified with orthodoxy in the mind of the modern Christian and is for that reason very difficult to correct. It is, for all its harmless seeming, a most injurious belief, for it destroys our sense of responsibility for our moral conduct. It robs all sin of its frightfulness and makes evil to consist in a mere technicality. And where sin is not cured power cannot flow.

Another doctrinal hindrance is the teaching that men are so weak by nature that they are unable to keep the law of God. Our moral helplessness is hammered into us in sermon and song until we wilt under it and give up in despair. And on top of this we are told that we must accept Jesus in order that we may be saved from the wrath of the broken law! No matter what the intellect may say, the human heart can never accept the idea that we are to be held responsible for breaking a law that we cannot keep. Would a father lay upon the back of his three-year-old son a sack of grain weighing five-hundred pounds and then beat the child because he could not carry it? Either men can or they cannot please God. If they cannot, they are not morally responsible, and have nothing to fear. If they *can,* and *will not,* then they are guilty, and as guilty sinners they will be sent to hell at last. The latter is undoubtedly the fact. If the Bible is allowed to speak for itself it will teach loudly the doctrine of man's personal responsibility for sins committed. Men sin because they want to sin. God's quarrel with men is that they will not do even that part of the will of God which they understand and could do if they would.

From Paul's testimony in the seventh chapter of Romans some teachers have drawn the doctrine of moral inability. But however Paul's inner struggle may be interpreted, it is contrary to the whole known truth to believe that he had been a consistent law-breaker and violator of the Ten Commandments. He specifically testified that he had lived in all good conscience before God, which to a Jew could only mean that he had observed the legal requirements of the law. Paul's cry in Romans is not after power to fulfill the simple morality of the Ten Commandments, but after inward holiness which the law could not impart.

It is time we get straightened out in our thinking about the law. The weakness of the law was three-fold: (1) It could not cancel past sins—that is, it could not *justify;* (2) it could not make dead men live—that is, it could not *regenerate;* (3) it could not make bad hearts good—that is, it could not *sanctify.* To teach that the insufficiency of the law lay in man's moral inability to meet its simple demands on human behaviour is to err most radically. If the law could not be kept, God is in the position of laying upon mankind an impossible moral burden and then punishing them for failure to do the impossible. I will believe anything I find in the Bible, but I do not feel under obligation to believe a teaching which is obviously a mistaken inference and one, furthermore, which both contradicts the Scriptures and outrages human reason.

The Bible everywhere takes for granted Israel's ability to obey the law. Condemnation fell because Israel, having that ability, refused to obey. They sinned not out of amiable weakness, but out of deliberate rebellion against the will of God. That is the inner nature of sin always, willful refusal to obey God. But still men go on trying to get conviction upon sinners by telling them they sinned because they could not help it.

The vogue of excusing sin, of seeking theological justification for it instead of treating it as an affront to God, is having its terrible effect among us. Deep searching of heart and a resolute turning from evil will go far to bring back power to the Church of Christ. Tender, tear-stained preaching on this subject must be heard again before revival can come.

The contradictions observed in the teachings which we have examined here are another cause of weakness. Christians do not, as a rule, enjoy great power until they begin to think straight. Whether or not the Methodists were right on every point they held is an open question; but their leaders had thought things out so clearly that they were not leading the people around in circles. As far as they could see there were no contradictions in their philosophy of faith, and this was a source of real strength to them. The same was true in the Finney revivals. God used Finney to get people thinking straight about religion. He may not have been correct in all his conclusions, but he did remove the doctrinal stalemates and start the people moving toward God. He placed before his hearers a moral either/or, so they could always know just where they stood. The inner confusion caused by hidden contradictions was absent from his preaching. We could use another Finney today.

6

Through the Out-poured Spirit

A disinterested observer, reading without the handicap of doctrinal prejudice, would surely gather from the Scriptures that God desires to advance His work among men by frequent outpourings of the Spirit upon His people as they need them and are prepared to receive them.

We make this statement with the full knowledge that it will be hotly challenged by some teachers. "It is not scriptural," they say, "to pray for or expect an outpouring of the Spirit today. The Spirit was poured out once for all at Pentecost and has not left the Church since that time. To pray for the Holy Spirit now is to ignore the historical fact of Pentecost." That is the argument used to discourage expectation, and it has been successful in damping down the fervor of many a congregation and silencing their prayers. There is a specious logic about this objection, even an air of superior orthodoxy; but for all that, it is contrary to the Word of God and out of harmony with the operations of God in Church history.

The Bible does not sponsor this chilling doctrine of once-for-all blessing. Rather, it encourages us to expect "showers of blessing" and "floods upon the dry ground." It was impossible for the outpouring which came at Pentecost to affect persons who were not present or congregations not yet in existence. It is obvious that the spiritual benefits of Pentecost must be prolonged beyond the lifetimes of the persons who were the first to receive them. The Spirit must fill not only that first company of "about an hundred and twenty," but others as well, or the blessings of that experience would cease with the death of the last member of the original band.

All this seems reasonable enough, but we have a more sure word of Scripture: Some time after Pentecost a company of believers met to pray for strength and power to meet the emergency then facing them, and to enlist the help of God on their behalf. "And when they had prayed, the place was shaken where they were assembled together; and they were all filled with the Holy Ghost, and they spake the word of God with boldness" (Acts 4:31). Some of these were of the original number filled at Pentecost. It is hardly conceivable that God acted contrary to His own will in filling them again *after* Pentecost. Still other outpourings are recorded in Acts 8, 10 and 19. All these occurred some years after the original act.

In brief, the teaching of the New Testament is that the outpouring at Pentecost was the historic beginning of an era which was to be characterized by a continuous outpouring of the Holy Spirit. Through the prophet Joel, God had promised that He would, during the last days, pour out His Spirit upon all flesh. The phrase "the last days" applies to a period beginning with the first advent of Christ and continuing through to the second. This is the position held by Dr. C. I. Scofield, as may be learned from his notes on Joel 2 and Acts 2.

That God's promise of poured-out power is meant for the Church for the whole time of her earthly warfare is confirmed to us by the recorded experiences of 1900 years. While Christendom as a whole has been content with creed and form, there has always been a smaller group within the larger body which has proved the promises and enjoyed the fruits of Pentecost. Powerful movings called "reformations," rushes of missionary activity, sudden breakings out of revival flame over communities and nations have been the sign of the fire by night to indicate the goings forth of God. In fairly recent times, as history goes, these spiritual visitations have given us the Moravians, the Methodists, the Salvation Army, and a galaxy of mighty preachers and missionaries whose names are in the Book of Life. In these very days in which we live there are scattered evidences that God is still pouring out His Spirit upon men. The mighty works taking place in the Scandinavian countries, in the East Indies and in French Indo-China can be explained only as new chapters in God's unfinished book, the Acts of the Holy Ghost.

Now, if God wills to pour out His Spirit upon us, why do not more Christians and more churches receive an experience of power like that of the early Church? That some have so received is joyfully admitted, but why is the number so few? When the provision is so broad and the promise so sure, what doth hinder us?

In answer, we present the following analysis, which, if no more, has this much to its credit, that it is the fruit of painstaking and prayerful observation.

One obstacle to the reception of power is a widespread fear of our emotions wherever they touch the religious life. This has gone so far that it has become a phobia with many serious-minded people. Men who should know better will kneel for an hour beside a seeker, all the time warning him against his emotions as against the devil himself. Bible teachers declaim against feelings till we are ashamed to admit that we ever entertained anything so depraved. Feeling and faith are opposed to each other in modern teaching, and the listener is given to understand that any exhibition of emotion is indelicate, if not carnal, and should be avoided at any cost.

This anti-emotionalism, though it is sponsored by some good people and travels in pretty orthodox company, is nevertheless an unwarranted inference, not a scriptural doctrine, and is in violent opposition to psychology and common sense. Where in the Bible are feeling and faith said to be at odds? The fact is that *faith engenders feeling as certainly as life engenders motion.* We can have feeling without faith, it is true, but we can never have faith without feeling. Faith as a cold, unemotional light is wholly unknown in the Scriptures. The faith of those Bible heroes listed in the Book of

Hebrews invariably aroused emotion and led to positive action in the direction of their faith. A statement, a promise, a warning always produced a corresponding excitation of feeling in the heart of the believer. Noah was "moved with fear." Abraham "rejoiced" and "obeyed." The Book of Acts is almost hilarious with joy. Perhaps the best summary of the whole thing is made by Paul when writing to the Romans, "For the kingdom of God is not meat and drink; but righteousness and peace, and joy in the Holy Ghost." And Peter says, "Believing, ye rejoice with joy unspeakable and full of glory."

Another hindrance is fear of fanaticism. Instinctive revulsion from fleshly excesses and foolish undisciplined conduct on the part of some who profess lofty spiritual attainments has closed the door to a life of power for many of God's true children. They have been too refined to endure the coarse gaucheries and bad taste of those self-styled heirs of Pentecost. They have made the mistake of putting all teaching concerning the Holy Spirit in the same category, and consequently will have nothing to do with any of it. This is as much to be regretted as it is easy to understand. Such victims must be taught that the Holy Spirit is the Spirit of Jesus, and is as gracious and beautiful as the Saviour Himself. Paul's words should be kept in mind, "For God hath not given us the spirit of fear; but of power, and of love, and of a sound mind." The Holy Spirit is the *cure* for fanaticism, not the cause of it.

Another thing that greatly hinders God's people is *a hardness of heart caused by hearing men without the Spirit constantly preaching about the Spirit.* There is no doctrine so chilling as the doctrine of the Spirit when held in cold passivity and personal unbelief. The hearers will turn away in dull apathy from an exhortation to be filled with the Spirit unless the Spirit Himself is giving the exhortation through the speaker. It is possible to learn this truth and preach it faithfully, and still be totally devoid of power. The hearers sense the lack and go away with numbed hearts. Theirs is not opposition to the truth, but an unconscious reaction from unreality. Yet scarcely one of the hearers can tell another what the trouble is; it is as if they had been hearing an echo and not the voice, or seeing a reflection and not the light itself.

Then I would mention another thing which clearly hinders believers from enjoying the power of the Holy Spirit: It is the habit of instructing seekers to "take it by faith" when they become concerned with their need of the fulness of the Holy Spirit.

Now, it is a fact written all over the New Testament that the benefits of atonement are to be received by faith. This is basic in redemptive theology, and any departure from it is fatal to true Christian experience. Paul teaches emphatically that the Spirit is received through faith, and rebukes anyone who would teach otherwise. So it would seem, on the surface of it, to be sound procedure to instruct a seeker to "take it by faith." But there is something wrong somewhere. One is forced to wonder whether the words "by faith" mean the same thing when used by modern teachers as they did when used by St. Paul. A sharp contrast is observable between Spirit-filled Christians of St. Paul's time and many who claim to be filled with the Spirit today. Paul's converts received the Spirit by faith to be sure, *but they actually received Him:* thousands now go through the motion of taking Him by faith, and believe they do so take Him, but show by their continued feebleness that they do not know Him in real power.

The trouble seems to be with our conception of faith. Faith, as Paul saw it, was a living, flaming thing leading to surrender and obedience to the commandments of Christ. Faith in our day often means no more than a meek assent to a doctrine. Many persons, convinced of their need of power, but unwilling to go through the painful struggle of death to the old life, turn with relief to this "take it by faith" doctrine as a way out of their difficulty. It saves their faith and enables them to march along with the true Israel. But it is they who constitute the "mixed multitude" which slows down the progress of the Church and causes most of the trouble when things get tight. And unless they see it differently later and decide to go through the hard way, they are fated to spend the rest of their lives in secret disappointment.

Let it be remembered that no one ever received the Holy Spirit's power without knowing it. He always announces Himself to the inner consciousness. God will pour out His Spirit upon us in answer to simple faith, but real faith will be accompanied by deep poverty of spirit and mighty heart yearnings, and will express itself in strong crying and tears.

7

Unity and Revival

God always works where His people meet His conditions, but only when and as they do. Any spiritual visitation will be limited or extensive, depending how well and how widely conditions are met.

The first condition is oneness of mind among the persons who are seeking the visitation.

"Behold how good and how pleasant it is for brethren to dwell together in unity! It is like the precious ointment upon the head, that ran down upon the beard, even Aaron's beard: that went down to the skirts of his garments; as the dew of Hermon, and as the dew that descended upon the mountain of Zion: for there the Lord commanded the blessing, even life for evermore" (Psa. 133). Here the unity precedes the blessing, and so it is throughout the Bible. An individual may seek and obtain great spiritual help from God; and that is one thing. For a *company* of people to unite to seek a new visitation from God for the entire group is quite another thing, and is a spiritual labor greatly superior to the first. The one is a personal affair, and may easily begin and end with a single person; the other may go on to bless unlimited numbers of persons.

It can hardly be doubted that there are many Spirit-filled persons, living pure devoted lives, who nevertheless exercise little or no power in the direction of revival. They live in beautiful isolation, doing nothing to bring down "showers of blessing" upon the larger group. Such as these have given up to the spirit of the times and have ceased to expect revival tides. They hear Jesus say, "Let down the hook and line for a fish," rather than, "Let down the net for a draught."

There is such a thing as a flow of blessing, where one experience merges into another, one day's grace moves on to the next. The spiritual mood persists from one meeting to the next, permitting the Spirit to *advance* His work. It eliminates the discouraging necessity to repeat each Sunday the work done the week before. It gives the high benefit of accumulation and serves to attract increasing numbers to the fountain. It is this we need today.

Historically, revivals have been mainly the achieving of a oneness of mind among a number of Christian believers. In the second chapter of Acts it is recorded that they were "all with one accord in one place" when the Spirit came upon them. He did not come to bring them into oneness of accord; He came because they were already so. The Spirit never comes to *give* unity (though His presence certainly aids and perfects such unity as may exist). He comes to that company who have, through repentance and faith, brought their hearts into one accord.

This may disturb some who have not stopped to question the commonly accepted doctrine that unity of heart among Christians is a sovereign work of God, and that we can have no part in it. This dull doctrine of inaction has taught us that we should study to do nothing and hope vaguely that somehow God will bring us to oneness of accord. If the achieving of unity is solely a work of God, why are we constantly exhorted to unity by Christ and His apostles? "Fulfil ye my joy, that ye may be likeminded, having the same love, being of one accord, of one mind" (Phil. 2:2). "Endeavouring

61

to keep the unity of the Spirit in the bond of peace" (Eph. 4:3). "I beseech Euodias, and beseech Syntyche, that they be of the same mind in the Lord" (Phil. 4:2). "Now I beseech you, brethren, by the name of our Lord Jesus Christ, that ye all speak the same thing, and that there be no divisions among you; but that ye be perfectly joined together in the same mind and in the same judgment" (1 Cor. 1:10). It is plain from all this that believers have a large part in achieving and maintaining unity among themselves. In this as in everything else God must give effective aid, but He cannot do the work alone. He must have active cooperation on the part of the believer. And since the Holy Spirit can do His mighty works only where unity exists, it becomes of utmost importance that everyone who desires revival do everything in his power to bring about such a state of unity on as wide a scale as possible.

Now, it is easy to find in this teaching a source of discouragement for the struggling pastor. "If oneness of accord is so important to the working of the Spirit, then I despair of my church. Its members are made up of a cross-section of Protestantism, with a dozen shades of theological opinion among them. They agree on the fundamentals, it is true, but they differ on so many points that I could never hope to bring them together. How can they erase the differences arising from varying religious backgrounds? How can they ever see eye to eye on all points? If God cannot send refreshing until we have accomplished what I believe to be the impossible, then our case is hopeless." Something like this will be the reply to our exhortation to unity, and the troubled soul who thus states his case will be no opposer, but a sincere lover of God and men.

This argument would seem to destroy all that has been said in favor of revival unity were it not for two facts: (1) The oneness of which we speak is not theological oneness; (2) unity embracing one hundred per cent of the people is not required before God begins to work. God responds to even "two or three" who may be gathered in His name; the extent and power of His working will depend upon the size of the nucleus with relation to the total number of believers in the church.

Revival unity is not the same as doctrinal unity. God demands no more than oneness in *all things that matter;* in all other things we are free to think as we will. The disciples at Pentecost were one only in the things of the Spirit; in everything else they were one hundred and twenty. Harmony may be defined as oneness at points of contact. It need extend no further than this to meet the requirements of revival. God will bless a body of men and women who are one in spiritual purpose, even if their doctrinal positions are not identical on every point.

Then, we should be encouraged to know that God does not wait for perfection in any church. A smaller group within the larger body may be the key to revival. They who compose this group need only become united in heart and purpose and God will begin a work in them, a work which may go on to embrace larger numbers as they meet the simple conditions. The greater the number in any church who are of one heart and one mind the more powerfully will the Spirit move in His work of salvation; but He never waits for an every-member participation.

Every church should strive for unity among its members, not languidly, but earnestly and optimistically. Every pastor should show his people the possibilities for power that lie in this fusion of many souls into one.